This Army Cadets Notebook Belongs to

_____

Being an Army Cadet has a lot of benefits.
Take part in exciting challenges and activities
such as:

- Abseiling
- Adventurous training
- Archery
- Kayaking
- Mountain biking
- And many other sports

Also –

Military themed activities, for example:

- Field craft
- First aid
- Fitness
- How to work in a team, or alone
- Leadership training
- Navigation
- Self discipline
- Shooting and marksmanship
- Survival skills

Use this notebook to keep a record of your
progress or for general observations and notes.

Activities

Activities

Activities

Activities

Activities

Date _____

Activities

Activities

Activities

Activities

Date

Activities

Activities

Activities

Activities

Activities

Activities

Activities

Activities

Activities

Activities

Activities

Activities

Activities

Activities

Activities

Thank you for purchasing this note book.
This is a very useful and practical notebook/journal.
If you agree please would you leave a review on
Amazon, it would be greatly appreciated.

Printed in Great Britain
by Amazon

14684518R00071